Shift Gristle

Shift Gristle

Heller Levinson

Boston, MA

Black Widow Press is an imprint of Commonwealth Books,
Inc., Boston, MA. Distributed to the trade by NBN (National
Book Network) throughout North America, Canada, and the U.K.
All Black Widow Press books are printed on acid-free paper, and
glued into bindings. Black Widow Press and its logo are registered
trademarks of Commonwealth Books, Inc.

Joseph S. Phillips and Susan J. Wood, Ph.D., Publishers
www.blackwidowpress.com

Cover design: Linda Lynch
Layout: Kerrie Kemperman
Cover art: Linda Lynch, *Shift Gristle Stacked Stone,* graphite, pastel,
and watercolor on cotton paper, detail, 18 x 12 inches, 2022

ISBN-13: 979-8-9880852-0-1
Printed in the United States
10 9 8 7 6 5 4 3 2 1

Only in drawing language relentlessly towards the innermost core of its own innermost silence can we hope to attain a veritable effect. — Walter Benjamin

The essence of life is to be found in the frustrations of established order. The universe refuses the deadening influence of complete conformity. And yet in its refusal, it passes toward novel order as a primary requisite for important experience. — John Gardner, *Grendel*

There are certain truths which transcend the power of the intellect to grasp, which can only be conveyed by evocation. — Matthew Prichard

And the narrowest hinge in my hand puts to scorn all machinery. — Walt Whitman

for George Torok

VALVULAR ASH

wind-studded thought-wren

wrestles archaic

flips the lurch drive sudden

sodden of foot

of trough

OF A LOST MEANING

       sunk-ward   carapace

                                    shred

                                    shroud

      how much of/'meaning'/is/meaningless

pertinence ramps parataxic

borders dissolve

sulking at the base of an extended furlough, plaints from

the elf-garden, the tottering jungle gym, —

ruffling laminae maroon, pump skittish homilies in-

to frozen food, → foul

foundation, queasy outline

as if meaning were residential, were a

summary or a summons, foragers

scrap for edifice, institutions

intensify pile-up

stale contagion warps the dry bed

MOROSE

dappled orange the

color you cheated. eyes grey

with terminal chatter. reckless.

the load proffering

backward.

low to high with backward. petting precipitous over low flame. uproar.

voices dodge. weave wary. circumspection overwrought. trouser glean.

mowing as a form of culture. corner rooms. overhangs offer.

what.

be well slant. slightly. crease. nearly slow before the leap.

    with breath bolster. bolster boisterous. alms. ornamental basketry.

sine qua non. glissade. the piano with green keys.

                    faraway blue eyes.

                      squeal.

drying is a dull art. add tears. washboard. circumlocution. brevity

shadow long speeches adversarial. circumspect. sails aplenty. above

board.

glory days among.

his constitution was strong.

weary countenance trying.

perturbingly upright then clause. off to the left wing clear. unobtrusively. irregular. unfamiliar. faint. dark tribune. trebuchet. revocable hour. when honky tonk *un*-reigns. only so much combustion. so much restraint. temerity. seclusion. blankets. stars.

sunrise. melodious timbre sponge trellis. promises. songé. plausibility. countless hours.

destitution.

prepositionally before counterfeit. cheery nutmeg. lanterns across the bridge fondly tugboat humor roused the waters.

drilling more quiet.

succulent.

observationally a company of truants queer tendency beside the rain water firmament flare it was over before it was decided.

decreed. decreed & nothing.

   offalmildew   pestilence

cheerful at the ready doors swung open. swing to a crying. no hold

back. well-ups & downfalls.

dribble through conspiracy.

axiomatic legs.

on all fours. slink. pad.

         pour forth. headway. vitality

stirred. roughed up.   at the end of the

revolution.   begin. patter.

         pins   needles

            pond   petals

            how much of

            love

            is

memory

how much of/bipedal/is

tree

The light of old things, of beautiful old things, awoke in me.

— Sherwood Anderson

swathes wash-lift, titillative

    fibers twine through time,

        tangle through grasses, air,

           the storied

           the beheld

these old pliers, bruised, complacent,

loose, slackened by the exigencies

of labor, the perfume of application

seasoned armchair yellowing from

the fade of multitude, stuffed

with the mnemonics of repose, the

armature of provision

spattering through the long cornfields sacred vessels

spring alive, drink the oil of the

corn, flutter to the western winds

things patinated,

     foamingricketyhistorical,

flux-chugging

Linda Lynch, *Drawing for Sherwood Anderson*, pastel pigment and graphite on cotton paper, 22¹/₄ x 30 inches, 2022

circumambulation pressed to the floor of wander

        fibrillate   cauliflower junket

            overleaf   cloverleaf   shipyard

                aerospace

                community

root uprooted by regularity.

peevish ceremonials tribal

commiseration.

wend.

warp.

wrest.

tell them what you like, — I

am not home.

disappearances aside there is a

chilliness, an abrasion that tears, that convolutes into

heretic, into excoriate, a

time of license & regret, licentiousness

& curry. how long

will it take to

forget.

tales long buried ossification resistant three-eared troubly past due terms

the technology is inadequate the stress of times sharp corners spider wax

engine grummet company in arrears flag wave spirit makeshift has a way

of spinning clear out to reconsider rest room over there brief cavalier

satchel war lords bearing briefly the

matter is closed

circuitously need leaches privilege time-sulk caretaker cane crutch

upstart states that but for shod breeze scanty buzz parapatric speciation

earth of the mothers upon the shield welt ribbon skirt blaze overall high

heel frenzy charm bracelet or not bruise

repair

SAY.   speak sundry. from

well-up. down under. swell.

                                        storm.

in(still(stigate) . prick flame.

firmament.   ·   flare → →

say = prong = prow = _____.

plunge bellow.   plumb breath blow   ges tic u late .

gyre capacious.   decibel stew.   strew sonic.

slake. infiltrate. frond filigree

taut.

chamber

clamor

coruscate

Ambrosial Osmosis

peppering linden otherwise persuasion

    courting cool coral

reverberates splice the runway

PERCH

fend whip foil assuage go lively

      prosperity muck street hyperbole

      . position

      . loft

      . proprioception

contiguous babble courts fetches compliance

too many moons soil the siesta

by degrees, up slowly,

. . .

then hoist

CREVICE CURL

cloy to

abject

inadmissible

lull   a   by

frozen lute thaw

CROSSFELLING ENCOUNTER LADEN

with stone begins. unladen. ladling porous. punctuation free. curious

come nightly timely & unsubscribed. low numbers constitute incline.

flies the function. fiery fliers. fireflies. over there then.

yonder.

CROSSFELLING ENCOUNTER LODGE

lob mellow dissolve. univocity

pierce. dissemble with migratory intent.

adhere along the way amass

prone. collapse upside down erectility

veer. delicacies smitten.

pull the lever prompt.

CROSSFELLING ENCOUNTER LODE

permeable close before filing. on the heels of dearth recompense mere

expense. countertop proxy eerily taut drops finger foreheads early starts

presume daily hush tones clatter free.

pioneers in the pantry

whirlcaster

what?

shift gristle contagious hardly wear-

able corners contain miracles. bulk attracts accumulation early hour voices

unload politely. sandy beaches spill. perpetuity. absent

mindedly. aghast.

squallfrost

clam amber

stormfed

firewood

MODELING VERTIGO

wooze wobble discombobulate tremor-hand dissolute

     tumbleweed   snowfall   handrail

askant systems fail. calculation owes benevolence to fracture. to

inopportune encounter. adversity flail ruptures squashberry adamantine

melt.

droll dossier

perturbability

Shiver Pulp

gnash arousal   statutory pits facet lash

      rig brachiate   purl cellulosic

               feted ambrosia

               lunk ankle

               lank piccolo

scab mnemonics emblem wilt caress quotient caulk the call to arms was

overdue. blessed infantry.

               mud in your eyes.

noodling bellwether rumbustious rhom-

boid icicling downtown the

thrill is gone

among penitents this ardor

                                            this

squeeze-fletch pan-pursue gyral-sphere

anchorage   cartography   serendipity

rudder complex downstream ratamacue hyperbole

corner →

the grace note

the heart on stilts

riddles

HEDGE

rim rowel roué roust

    meridian mince

calibrations court the countryside laborious adventure advances undeterred.

        rumble-frost

        revelatory: the disappearance of welts

            : blackberry demise

canopy colossus sprint underling thresh-

hold spray

            idiosyncrasy

           rat-a-tat

      moon-cheat

the oblong

is hardly derivative

SLANT

stowing grackles the lantern pitches.

history slide: wheels come of age

it wasn't always like this,

      wayward, then abrupt, as

      if a grasp could take hold

grace notes trammel, despair

      pocks the stairwell, resistances

abide, it is not

time

Abyssal Roam

rut runner fodder eclipse tan-

tamount soluble

      storm faucet

      follicle tear

rumble roar adumbrate caliginous

dazzle, robust larch resin rich,

perplexity joust spasm departure infest, lowly

rudderless dim   diminishment plunge

abate

CHURN

the shape of things grew slumber

         slim firings lacerate

         abbreviation coils curtail

         color the garden party

abode-leaven draw the curtains

slippage informs through *through,* passage

as tender, fleet-mane

         ribaldry

scramble tesserae subvert root

matter

tales ambagious

nightly

BAMBOOZLE

fictive float   ruse

                sleight

flood intrigue

a formulation borderline, . . .

litotes

innovative insert

The Bamboozle Blossom departs in 20 minutes

Epileptic Altitude

in the *thickening* legume legitimacy yarns blister. culture atrophies with

distance.   footfalls.   whortbonker easelheist.   home-strung.

bruise-missile

careless scrolls

aphids aside sweep herald the season swears good. unfortunate if the

mould recedes . . .

clues bear calling

CALL

lurecast   vapourwreath   thirsttroll

        [not 'call' as in naming, but as

        that which is yet to appear →] →

to appear as summons →   dreamsough   crest-

ripple

        attire pulmonic

        leaven pore

        bell-throb-titillate

trilling nebulous troughs

latchless

the lariat slings

The *S*pray notes (s) are intended to irrigate the text much as a fine mist recirculates to sea.

S 'Call' Hinges to Heidegger's *What Is Called Thinking*. "The old word 'to call' means not so much a command as a letting-reach, that therefore the call has an assonance of helpfulness and complaisance, is shown by the fact that the same word in Sanskrit still means something like 'to invite.'"

APPEAR

cloak-thresh   aphotic-reel   pin →

wheel scrub   scroll gestate

                       eke

                       swell

              am   pli   fy

b   u   r   g   e   o   n

The appearing, under the mantle of approach, masticates distance,

succors a varietal of *near.*

wrest

contour

insinuate

S The appearing wells-up from the Call.

NEAR

needling approximate   frisson fidget

where in the/approach/is/

expectation

furl slur spatial accomplice   fissure-gapclunk

                    immanence beaches

the approximate gathers in the folds of accumulate   laplob

                                                  lipwhistle

                                        cleat-hop

in the bloom of assonant conflux propinquitous admix impels *for-ward*, …

to-*ward*

in presencing, the ardor of gather disappears.   gather conjugates

contiguity.

where in

abode

is

akin

in approximation

the near

consults

ACCUMULATE

in the raw compound of

concussive congenital

stacked

persuasion

S "Accumulate" extends the term 'accumulate,' found in the 6th line down of
NEAR (application above) & also Hinges to cover art by Linda Lynch.

ACCUMULATE

ramped preserve

agglutinate tower

bit by bit

hoard conspicuous

new

doesn't anyone say *glade* anymore?

WOEBEGONE

rib-wrack thrash temblor   rancid ratch

                                  saccharine infest

                                  putrid placidity

garroted to a lymph reprisal vermin prodigious hatch munch lively

                                  puncture animadvert

                                  umbelliferous decay

telltale subversion

the sorely told wallows

lashers-on scabrous breath sunk debt declivitous moil soul mire per-

emptory

scarified by the ornamental dead

rotting from an obscure infarction

shinnying the spine of

an ancient

appaloosa

LOST

atlas toss   Baedeker bruise   lit flint-

                                             cackle decibel moan

                                             corridor crackdown

                                             oblivion pardon

vertiginous mandible (cl)(qu)ench-qualm elab-

                                      orate

                             how ?

                             how to ?

                             where

                'why' cosseted in tundra quiver, glossed with

despair anvil turn-about

beyond the ridge?

'perhaps' becomes conclusive

                                      winds spoke the calendar, icicles

                                    prance

                                    twigs hunker nearly

the far-off reaches

ABODE

sonata siesta   Handel hammock   fit-ful-

ly strew splendor strain-less

                    repose

burden hearth release   syllable succulent

root: to root: route: to place

                    : rooted

              where in

              abode

              is

              saturation

chaos translates

wearing loose shapes   tidying-up

thing-nuzzle

filtrate

trace gases, dead galaxies

morning of heaves halves spike-slice fleshflense heart-

ache

sandpaper armpit

freshwater rot

hold the synopsis

ghoul conclusions cross the line ur-

gent get outta here comeuppance is in the mail

already sent

pocked tubas replicate

no awards bragged the wall

where are you going?

is there a satisfying moment?

a world without *is*　?

fire in the gully blues from the muddy blister maelstrom it's all in

how you say goodbye

grab a hold how unfortunate pulley rust EVACUATION is

the keynote speaker

> I'm interested in the long form <

. autocrine misfire

. orbital debris

. rancid penguin tongue

alkaptonuria = black piss disease → wets

the land

where can I buy a 'sweet dream' ?

'21 Days of Calm

Integrate Mindfulness into your everyday life'

into my every*night*

my menopause

my premature ejaculation

Fuck Calm!

pursuing advanced studies in Gyration buckling the shoes assumes a

higher significance

assigned to hunt for 'surety,' I pause with Su Shi by the cherry blossoms

Can I walk you to school?

floccinaucinihilpilification

Neils Bohr: How wonderful that we have met with a paradox. Now we

have some hope for making progress.

                    how much of

                    hysterical

                    is

                    farcical

solve 'hysterical' as if it were a mathematical problem

conjugate hysteria

he was told it would come hard & fast

the forgotten doesn't forgive

are you tired of subways too?

adam/eve

I wish it were that simple

do/don't

plunge or stay dry

You seek the company of cards?

Really?

clever is not enough

'too easy' lacks endurance

empty boasts lack colorful dresses

while you were out dancing the spokes got wet

Deborah I love you. with an all-consuming love. love-

consumed vanishes in the vast vault of the

appetitive.

Deborah, my love got lost.

whereabouts is where?

vacation in the wasteland

           'life has taken a bitter turn'

           'you don't say'

        the supposed wakes a

           wend   a faltering

             verisimilitude

no kid left behind

when rudiments lose their way

        pick-up-sticks

          more wrist action

it didn't have to be like this

          how much of

          the cloud

          is

          cloudy

spread sheets grow uneasy

traffic has stopped

currencies glut in the cloud

trade has halted

in the morning there was a new god

WALL WEEP VICTUAL

loop largesse   nu-

trients pocketed brought aboard

savvy salve mood madness glandular

deck wash

                    scrub affix

mortar smelts

the 'remark'

tucks away

WEFT WHARF GARDEN

purblind   ailing with exceptional cunning, assiduous learning,

rapid-fire calculation,

: station serrate dentulous shift :

the beast unloads, bracket pilfer io-

dine

: dinner was timely though lacking nutrients :

across the board the vision was applauded, confirmed, . . . vast profits

visualized

venture bestir bed Bedouin trance

harbinger sheetrock

cleats for footing

forethought serves

foresight serves better

walk the dog/pick-up sticks/dishes

around 1275 to 1324 (when the first mechanical clock was built)

counting assumes precedence

cosset angel lash loom lugubrious

maggot fund persiflage

the illustrious fade, sustain putrefies

where is the ambush?

if we knew we'd be gods

MOLLIFY   MELLIFLUOUS   ADHESIVE

. durable

. drainage

. dregs

UTTERLY

utter twined, utter, prime phonate, churnChaw grind deLIBerate upcharge

from *uter* "outer," swell sonic shape

> where in the

> sound

> is the

> proposition

yowl forth urge/grate into being, outlash into the 'open'

open: compass collapse

> providential invite

HEED

extravasate   prime

                       focus forthright

                       interlock

              in-hale

plump   billow conspicuous

                       motley shadow carouse

                       eidetic reduce

smithe savvy   sieve   source scurry

                                        ↓

                               longitudinal wobble

                                        ↓

                               horizon heist

                                        ↓

                               arterial vessel

                     celerity conjunct

: is heed mere paying attention? does

Husserl's *epoché* – bracketing

phenomena with suspended judgement

– enable approach? :

how much of

the

reel-in

pre-supposes

dew-lipped lapidarian concourse scuttle chisel ladder precipitous

peel dross

lance fructuous

scrutinize

on

toward

ever

querulous

feeling

palpable obscure

shroud smother carom mist envelop

                                  canopies plethoric, expelled

                                  visible

    the

        blissful no condition but stone

shortchange the wobble concerns

overdue not the least hitch to

neighborhood [lodestar megacenter Madagascar]

where 'near'

                tides/tidies

                    un-

wrinkles

the abyss

ROVE

      indent   lanyardlobkeel

                traipse

            proboscis lumber

histography   ornithology   diaper rash

            lacunae leap

      ash legato   ramble alliterate

            acro-

batics hard of hearing a wet well well wet a mouthful   swallow paths a

way

                              : microbial decency

                              : asymptotic straggle

                              : storage

in the company of lords

dereliction between tones

hike

in the precinct of lunk

       obdure

       abjure

       klunk oblong

cultivate incivilities confetti promiscuous

                    odds are it happens when

                    you aren't looking

mean-calculus gruel-flung spur-tied claustrophobic cowboy

back in what saddle?

      saddle: what back?

           where to?

     Hi-Yo Silver *!*

zombie infested device driven zeitgeist

show me your nightmare

carrion-gloat glut garrulous,   Algorithm, →

can you coin an anthem, pluck a lyre?

                          & the walls came tumbling

                                came tumble

sod travail ash dung born brummagem cast pernicious steeped toxic, ... heed →

coastal lemures slosh

Surplus

seizures   *vibrate*

You.

there. forthwith. unrealized. barren. empty of contour, of establish.

rigged to register, configure. orient.

> confabulate reckless reconsider long term
>
> parking fling partake assert yourself the
>
> summer lags

binomial fugue:

> what I make of you

> what you make of yourself

>> how much of

>> you

>> is

>> yourself

you circumnavigate, toss, cast long,

buoy bound,

quest driven,

rived to overbite you stall with calendric, seek the sensible to save you.

you underinflate your tires for winter,

prepare root vegetables.

steered by image gulps breathless the airing gropes. sure-footed is often

uninspiring. bled on its own dimension, the fan-out under performs.

in the rabid pronoun ricochet the cleat conjunction disappears, —

bounding to we   they   us   our, ... me .... the dissolving self reconstitutes

in the other, stakes out ventilatives, ... bramble dodge.

                    to compass a fragile earth

                    you wore bright clothes,

                    consumed lumps of vinegar

pick-up sticks this is America

everyone deserves a second chance

~   ~

you favored light & then, abruptly, you didn't. you fled the withers of

radiation, were inclined to burrow, to sink into shadow. shades were

pulled. lights dimmed. you pressed toward interiors. toward edges.

distanced yourself from outlets. lookouts. your dress changed to darks,

more moody, . . . loose. your speech too. once verb-spiced. lively. now

mostly lazy prepositions. inert. void of reference. of of.

it pains me to ask but:

are you Ok?

the above question subterfuges. I really want to know if I am losing you.

will you be gone. absent. a fraction of your former self. this centers

around me. will I be unable to receive what I need from you. what I cherish. how could I cherish you if what I cherish centers around what you provide me? is this duplicitous? or are all relationships provision instruments. equipment centers. fueling stations.

distraught. distraught feels, well, distraught. that is how you expressed it. after your plans collapsed. each plan seemed laced with hope. as if success would insure a more robust, enriched you. plans that struck-out would reduce, . . . as bricks removed from edifice.

perplexity-besieged you relied upon others to shape you. tracking their feedback this way that way, . . . perhaps, maybe.

peek-a-boo I see you.

do I?

do you?

PERPLEXITY

gnarly

breach

splendor

,

marigold

collards

conjunct smithereens boogie

;

M i s t

s

hump   lumber

ing

where in the

mist

is

violence

where in the

mist

is

murmur

how much of

mist

is

wishful

among: alouette

holiday piercings

afterthoughts of the left behind

!

buttercup

medley

inspiration

TORQUE

advanced ebullience   crank amplify

         axial bulge

squeeze through accelerate tube damask sparrow birch flee

         prong perpendicular

         gravitas gyrate

         tensile twist

         toggle thrust

spasm frantic vibrato

flutterrudderbutterfly

ERRANT

dislocate   list disquiet, .. err ...

shape in the pouch of leopard

               sluice-wind

   enter-prise

seize commission stature acquaint accomplish plummet plumb the

hidden, the lure-drenched obfuscations, skirl

salubrious bevel-slice brave

statute

skid

pad lively

pare

parse

omnivore

NETHER

undulate warp

wrangle flux

miasmatic

Trouble Is

currents alone   couldn't   won't   wouldn't   doesn't

account for windswept timber sulfur sprint soulful calamity jane cascade

say yes to reason to augment to flibbertigibbet dismissal count stars lie

awake introspect suspect yr mother drug rudder hyperbole axis advance

sniffles jujube trials wishful thinking willful junction traverse crisscross

accelerate bricolage more breakfast juice work the brakes find puppy a

home fill to full

ignore all this

good luck

lop fizzle

lope

lizardly

DISJUNCT

wrench coalition yank upheave

slice

duodenum ditch

overly concerned with performance gap-gall hieroglyphic hijack, numerical

singe, entreaty, cloud smelt tornado cinders

arbitrage

cleave

demote

hysteria unravel immiscible spew

maroon

chopped metaphors slop the bayou

chopped metaphors slop the bayou

coruscate idle geometry flunk

belly laughs iterate lodge

stale shingle

                              home comforts

                              reminiscence

                              quilt corrode

divaricated warlord dank ivory juxtapose spur

handicrafts unload the locksmith fustian aubade drag baton come

lightly trip gaily grab a tune cauliflower love-

ly

count

count backward

spin

c   a   v   o   r   t

[BRACKET

shore-up   [[[[support

                    [em

          [pha

                                                    sis]]]

lim]

                                    [Lim

it]

                                          [en

                                                            ]

gagglegoggledandydoodledangle dumpster proof wharf rodent

perforate rally chime chum perihelion personality modus operandi

prickle trickster fix-it rubbing alcohol sincerity the company of fishes

perfectly tuned what is the best polish for a willow violin for a sunset for

insect wings salami a bad attitude high turnover prevents excellence

pride of Cincinnati culled for brevity for interdisciplinary eroticism the

old folks at home once upon a time the clock is running abatement in a

low key wouldn't it be nice lonesome blues Diddie Wa Diddie oh this

diddie wa diddie on a clear day jump at the opportunity take it to the

max not a moment to arbitrate upon consider the middle road where

there's a perturbation will a way next page wish you were here horizon

for a penny tumbleweed tony do the math win a few lose a middle name

above board yours truly with a little bit study the small print seriously

too much too soon the trouble with finches chant blossom gaunt

cartoon given a chance

if only

when

Exploded Footnote

smithereens   legend smear

                        evacuate

                fracas blast

incinerate inert divisive tubes, subdivisions, enumerations, clogged duct,

failed filtration

                              (spore anemone sigil sluicetranspire

shatter the desperation-powdered viscid collectives pledged to stale

metrics, reeking

formulaic, →   carotid clunk

                    trellis crack

              gutted anemic

topple numerical tanks rutted to terrestrial bungle,

                      (vent original migration

rouse the polliwog pools, the plash arboreal,

lopside   unspecify   free range

wrack

sport a tune

WAY

tread   fringe lap   daredartdextrous

          pursue

court the loins of buoyancy, the

          errant fibrillations, the

          fibrous pedigree

a-fumble with perennial jockeying spill accumulations bulb nimbus mist

leaven spray marigold berry the flint whistle nimble, ... clamor quill, . . .

concertina

whiploads ferry the blue blister

to rail the long rupture delve deep vase dawns

WAY

stampede

clutch the rural song

GLOOM

glommed lugubrious gunk-coated sullen lark

                                    tar

                misgivings

peppered to obsolete logarithms solar-shudders shrivel rotational virility,

                                            capsize motility,

scuppered by the carboniferous bunk of an occluded legacy ill-advisements

crud canker corrode,

un-

pack

gutted centripetals

Trouble Is

crud coated gnash afflicted fusillade frenzy all aboard steamroll satanic

shimmy praxis flummox fungi parade   goo–wrapped gum-bubbled

atrocity riddled bloat blob   rash doom-driven panic blear   this

funk you can't debunk

drool gangrenous cumulative   abort contort cut along the dotted line

be besot cranky ill at sorts it takes all kinds days like this take 2 take 3 up

for grabs aquamarine terracotta pit stop downfall home improvement

leprous idle there must be some way outa here sidle slip slide hyper glide

blitz blizzardblink tincture loss where's the boss rat skunk skittle ladle

cap a top throne a bone

fancy

yrself

HYOID

centerpiece scalloped for speech, cry of the aurochs, tectonic twist, bulge

& belch

> [The evolution of lactation was instrumental in shaping the
>
> throat to speak as well as to feed.]

alluvial channel curve

eat ://: speak

mother's milk = articulation's upright bass

> [No reptile can suck.]

nutritive boost campfire quirk crater emblematic blaze fortuitous flame

vocal

> [The only bone in the body not connected to any other bone.]

lavish incidentals lurk larynx lump langoustine sea whelp, underwater

convolute, congregate,

cherrying the rails of a disputed synchronicity redeem the

lost decibel

the

cut tongue

BROOD

bred inclement   (indecency hive a brood a-way

                    spun gravitational

                    hark maroon, discolor

                    ash-feather

                    ashcurdle

lugubrious bedfellow spring sag sunk

undertone kingdom failure. bellies

come horde the hunt for brindle birdcaged

a day away.

crow gash in the exhume of mitigated flesh

vigil slant accents crop curry uneasily

churn

burnish

in the trundle swell of rinsed erudition

torpor toll   null bedfellow

                vapid ventral

pillow the warrants adhesives adhere surface circumstantial especially

suspect. leaky promissory notes. watch the ears when breaking a horse.

stop reading the news. margins are hirsute & terminal.

the unreliability of chimes beleaguers

make no sense of this

ease easily in the mellifluous ointment swirl eerily

disappearance

vessels pour the mainland

errancy ruled the tribe

no wrong way

MIST

flotation

mull

d   i   s   s   i

p   a

t   e

I hate old people.

STILL LIFE

quilsweep languish quiescent glove per-

turb

in-still

                          shape

                                    purge

                         predicate

                                    porous

                quell ex-

                trinsic

loose a

muffled

infinity

FLOWERS

double-handled pewter vase

flowers

7 roses

umbilicating

VASE

contour   sweep

    lapwavelapundulate

           ir-ri-desce

           accumulate

    warp venerable

    swellin-cline

s   *w*   *e*   *l*   *l*

     transit volume

             poise

             liquidity

endow   contain

where in the

vase

is

beckon

ERRANT

mis-placed   miscreant   out-

of-step   controversial   faulty from

fire that disinclined

from

plates that clash severe

        or

        not at all

Shadow Transliterate

raspless primed of bounce the jollity wayfares, trunktrails a foreshortened

itinerancy . . . .

                                                 purpling

                                       perplexion

                             mimesis

unraveling vibratories scroll the spine litter limbus

                           unseemly

                               disquiet

circumference voided the

breath abates,

tucks into pulmonary

miscalculation

isn't it

Chopped Metaphors Slop The Bayou

reel low grind drizzle gist trawl

                        ancient mnemonic subalterned

                        grasshopper fawn flute

the convoy of eerily

beauty prize suspend

rhinestone pluck

'I'm ancient as never before this afternoon,

charged with karstic urge, fully born.'

born frolic spray dolphin fire   finance-goblins cinder

preferendum queen of spades some-

way outta here

      trespass

      the property of perfect rotundity smithereens

      blow through blockage   sonic restraint

lexiconic stasticity   sing lyre

bumble bee   carnivore   leaf

strain minced signifiers through the perfume of

lentisk & terebinth   peddle collapse   mucous munitions

                                        transparent idle

copperhead fangs the verb

hush money

this   this

                    this

so   whereupon

                    behold

if   when

                        whereabouts

JUDDER

speckle garden lightfoot which way about face turn ahead frivolity

gumption castaway cliff hang flummery beacon bright scratch comply

adjectives slalom black diamond alphabet soup contrivance   comeuppance

castration   collection   curls for the hell of it first place slide to bass flung

otherwise orphan new shoes slip toward Singapore the refrain is deafening

clank clutter Wabash Cannonball the ease the simplicity wheel congeal

free for all crankshaft gasoline axle apple juice call

when you get there

SCUDDER

riprim   curlcoil   skimshimmy

                slither slide

                glitter glide

STUTTER

valvulate well-up, heave thwart, shiver reprise,

shuttered between bleak pincers, squeezed sullen, gated,

nod to barely, a curdle that just maybe . . . brick-

chested, pressed between the eaves of a false consummate, trowel

precipitous, overbear dodge, shirk

grandstand, crag-shift . . .

postures of malinform, bled munitions,

scratch,

fade,

paw through

Rural Songs from the Gunboat

sweet wheeze ka → boom

                  pikeberry lullaby

                        sunflower

ether loiter   troll transcendence

in the riparian quench of a stalled orthodoxy

                                    glut-clot

                                        lapidification

edges toy beginnings

soil plum(b)s porosity

declawed serenades sprinkle the field,

flake-offs from dispirited mechanisms, tuneless, blunt, root

res-

idential, roil whereabouts, consider plantings

the hurt fled otherwise

song

sycamore

the night sky

even so

whereupon the dark rang ferocious forecast falter felony

upbeat melody plea fidelity quell threnody days like this proper attire

propel pinch a beat crash a cymbal starlit bowsprit turnabout heave heave

come to me cleave(oh *cleav*-age) my darling pluck a'here pluck there turps

rubout scrub on all fours floorboard scratch squeak ploan moan

yesterday's clothing even under the radar pathos visible has a way unerring

divisibility surmise come as you are watch for seepage planetary rotation

is indistinguishable from Buddhism (?) in & out burger gas prices

counting shades of confinement perpetuity complex liner notes the leaves

are raspberry blush when counter clockwise cluck cluck cluck pass the

buck whine a shoe drill a hole kill a mole feather fright molt delight the

earth is a cube the earth is not a cube sheaf theory establishes reliability

over & over again rhapsody senility come as you are duplicitous

contraband controversial conundrum crux buster sums on board come

out come trip the meter fret the reaper where's the speaker nevermore

forevermore more's the least of it how shallow amplitudinously remote

grab a hold hold a hand grill a chill steal a shovel what comes from the

earth returns to the earth so says tracking data attached to the open sets of topological space hi ho hi ho ringalevio   approaching finality the

end of world history at this late stage of things *during* this late stage of

things how to conduct oneself? . . . . the

question lodged in dilemma. not a clue. this way, → push pull pulley lever

scramble brake accelerate more/less perhaps/maybe monkey wrench

quench down the trench if then where when

why

why not

PORE

see as thing the intervals between things themselves

— Merleau Ponty, *Phenomenology of Perception* (2002, 18)

OED: A. opening in the skin or body surface of an animal

B. a minute interstice between particles of matter

C. duct or passage

orifice debouche   coagulate   invite

where unformulation privileges formulation

— intrigue trigger

— cavernous fibrillate

the *in-between* preens as the unspoken for, as the emptiness

tuning adjacency, . . . antiphonal commingle, tendril

titillate

pore: possibility-packed

hole: penetrate or pour out from

space: offers → shape, or, adapt as required

where in the   how much of

empty   empty

is   is

navigation   navigable

rutting in ambidextrous roughage the yet-to-be slurs,

                                                    capers amid,

                        pinwheel probe

                        brew broth

plait pixie twirl loom extract bore

into, torque crank contort,

open, o p e n i n g s, . . . interosculate suffuse

                        interstitial itch

"The spaces between the particles of solid material are just as important to

the nature of the soil as are the solids themselves. It is in these *pore* spaces

that air and water circulate, roots grow, and microscopic creatures live."

where in the pore is the extractable?

can the extractable be the unidentified? the

shadow's marrow?

in the throttle-luxate-vein-crackle-roll, pores pepper the poem

onomatopoeia

    bumptious

      propagate

        gristle

shift to the archeology of wisdom, to the rim rouse

of the damp hollow, the

over/under turn

lips pulsate in the

sagacity of incompletion,

in the sultry caul

of

enormity

in the sheer shimmer hush rim

motile sluice, . . . *Abyssal*

Rouse ,   stir curry

                    clench claw

jam phantasm feint

indiscretion cull

grunt paw

the physics of export   (saddles of skin

(stirrups of tears

diurnal twist

dislodge

Abyssal Dislodge   run

amok   reel totter   rip-

      tide

prick   careen

cartwheel bobs feather plaster

MIST   RHYTHM   WONDER

        bobcat curl tender

tendril stump brief aporia enterprise

                                  spill

                    fume reduction

long legs blonde running oracular tongue terp-

                            sic-

                                hore

key elusive

orange

LIST   WOBBLE   RECKLESS

heretofore

preamble stumble upon the

takeaway coy-trenchant periwinkle unfold

                              reliability lapse

                              rhombus spun

                              quoit fever

                    (arrears

                    (governing powers

                  (obeisance

the company of lords calamity fastened what can the matter be

pursuant to our investigation

full compliance would be appreciated

                              nonetheless

                              furthermore

balance contests dislodge

                    how much of

commotion

is

arbitrary

adjective added

slippery when wet

MIASMA   MUDDLE   MEDDLESOME

. country roads

. briar

. privilege

WOBBLE   EXTRACT   PERTINACITY

. rudiment

. exertion

. outcome

REMOTE   SERENDIPITY   AMORPHOUS

. surprise

. sudden

. epiphany

BEAUTY TIP

Give your

cheekbones a rosy

glow by tapping

on Estee Lauder

Pure Color Envy

Sculpting Blush in

Pink Tease ($48)

SCAFFOLD

bulk-up raise

give lend to

contiguous co-opt

a construction constructing

subordinate or coordinate?

confer ://: defer

the humanity of the scaffold rests with its removal

Rubbed Omission

by which each

    thing   scrubbed tender,

rinsed lustral, unto its   sign-

auspicious, is

        rendered, →   filial burst

darts   fissures

reeds

rockfish

    & crystals, the blown circuits

of an advanced iconography

hush lacunae shift in the bladder

of time,

waves newly yet again & again newly,

                throne concupiscence,

                    idyll

outlay   upswell

crepitant seizures ballasted in cryptobiotic lingua bur-

row pores, festoon goblets, pour mischievous irrigators across airloft lather

where

eons conspire with eons, calibrate

stories of dirt, . . .   passage,

itself a ward,

in the filigree of extension, where

early sprout chips

through rubbed omissions,

foams

beneath

the

gnarl

~

whittled thin,

    poised evaporate,

debased to subliminal extraction,

      the words salve,

      incandesce,

        lusty

        floral

          through

throats of ancient stone, en-

during logjam & igneous mute,

obdurate with beguile, triggering

headwinds against the jawed rattle of

rigged inclines, *in-*

clined fibrillate, ambidextral, hinged,

web-

bed

to the perfume of

lentisk & terebinth

to

the strigilated ecstasies

of

vanishing trill

among the ruminants,

                          thistle flush

                                 morning warble

                                         sessility breach

sparingly, approximations gleam contour,

                  render inclination,   trimmed

           to outpost, to banner-prep,

to the naming that resists name,

that identifies through a scrolled vacuity,

through

silences threshing

in the armature

of

innuendo

~

to churn,

        to well-out

in frenzy-whip the faltering

steps *across,* convinced now

of *otherwise,*

diminutions overturn

in the harvest

of

adjusted light

THIS

singled out   pressed

alert, sprung

deliberate, . . . squeezed

browsing postures fret to assume

              the lug of initiation

              the suds of eke-out

THAT

thar

plucked

spot lit

spelled

Mollusk Phlegm

discourtesy rankles the haberdasher

closes his door   aperture skew

                        bumptious roar

titillates soft padding enterprise squid an

invigorated biology

overlooking a collapsed economy squirt bellows

Venetian red dominates   churl batter

                                                castigate

empty of options compromise coats

the corridors. maneuvers once facile now ungainly, shackled to a furrowed

tide, a wrinkled toxicity. when wet, clay is sticky & can be easily molded.

flutter quiver

        quill frisk

proceed

slipstream confetti flier extrap-

olate gorge extremity knot amplifiers early dispatch redundancy pile-up

vortex pluck caesura float faraway *therefore* as pronoun role adjust wide

lapels eel pastiche the trouble with averages is averages the trouble with

percentage is bring me little bourbon Sylvie suitable floral arrangements

quiet the tantrums overuse atrophies the lost art of repair how much

of the new is worn down with nothing new from sea to shining sea

abut abridge abort pernicious has no place in this sandwich yellow

submarine yellow

submarine

often overheard at/from/in guttergardengunshop cult committee

apostrophe belly kitchen cornpone parade baseball halls of gather glitter

clump function fructify merriment abates simile soufflé lopsided

discouragement x factor y tomorrow fortuitous overture lifestyle choices

pave the road button the chimney Blue Rondo a la Turk the young at

heart future belongs to opposing densities flotation a lost art the science

of repair appaloosas chew frightful melody come hither lately loosen your

dalliance occasionals in blotch pink readymade saddle collapse spur inert

court bridge gap the way of the rise furlough hi-5's the future's uncertain

multiple choice

where in the

gaze

is

swarm

SWARM

skittle burst scatter combust sling palaver   idle glide

                                              skit along fling

           multiples   rpm's   rev

revelate   from velocity this disarm

                momentous purr away

SWARM

sprint spirit spread sluice outlay   di-

versify   splash plural

throng plush pepper

gather congest skit spray

murm-ur-ate

prolificate

amplify

SWARM

castoff percolate enormity heave-throws heft

driven wound in ventricular helium at the base of slippage

spool velocity cascade uplift cocoon undulate spiral bound

oath airing a singular voice meticulously

elaborate

colloquial boon atmosphere bluff

residuals let the

weather decide isolation has

its utensil cheese is not

an occupation

OFFAL LOAD GROTESQUE

heinous spike peduncle fracture ordure ramp   com-

pounding decimates rattle erupt

foulspittlerancidrouse

    contaminate

    cantankerous corrupt

spooled through the drool of bilious →

    an abscess nation rolled putrescent, skank

    routed,

        depletive,

            sphacelating

By Amber Light

guileless the plot endures plucked of discomfort steeled zealous revels

gambol ubiquitous undergird blade strop fanfare strip down thunder lips

cumulous slalom curve   applause read rapture bop Rhythm-a-

Ning ling ding dong-a-ling ding do the dog the monkey the sassafras too

furry curry flavor nutmeg *nec-*

ta-*rine*

tell me

tell me

tell me

don't wait

WIND

does wind wind-up?

amass its forces before the unleash?

'Wind is air in motion. It is caused by uneven heating of the
atmosphere by energy from the sun.'

disturbance

how much of

disturbance

is

formative?

is

havoc?

Paul Blackburn: *I am a wind on the deep waters*   .

The wind that drives the floods   .

Beryl sea-green is the stone   .

Dwelling secure in the hollow

ship until

      wind wafts him home

Clear is the color of the wind in the

      aspen (white

        poplar)

is the wind weedless?

    wordless?

syllables contralto mush lullaby lyre the

wind, footprint the sun

        where in the

        wind

        is

        embark

      bellows/

        nautical/

          ahoy

Charles Olson: *It was the west wind caught her up, as*

                  she rose

                  from the genital

                  wave, and bore her from the delicate

                  foam, home

                  to her isle

wind irruptive, contemplator of measures

Wind travels because of air pressure.

Does placidity nullify the excursion?

        'The calm belt of air near the equator is called the *doldrums*.'

doldrums

seized   towed   pulley-leash draw

             furrow-slung

             clunk

             gravel lard

drugged immerse

bled sienna strings flail to wood, seek instrumentation

mulligrubs

stalled in the horse latitudes

        dolorous

            dry

wilt-

ing

What is the difference between breeze & wind?

is breeze Mozart & wind Wagner?

        or

breeze = Morandi   wind = Van Gogh?

a hop, skip, & a jump to

windfall

S 'Wind' also appears in *Query Caboodle.* This double appearance is considered re-*situating* rather than repeating. It is to highlight how an application appears differently under differing circumstances. As a rose in one section of a garden will evoke differently than a rose in another section.

ATOMIC NUPTIAL

blear batter rag   tatter folly

    upwell fetter fling

on all fours the principle is peace

        (warring is for the dogs

ceremoniously dress your heart appropriately

the seven headed trance certifies

    union is precarious

    isolation is unreliable

we're all fucked

HEFT

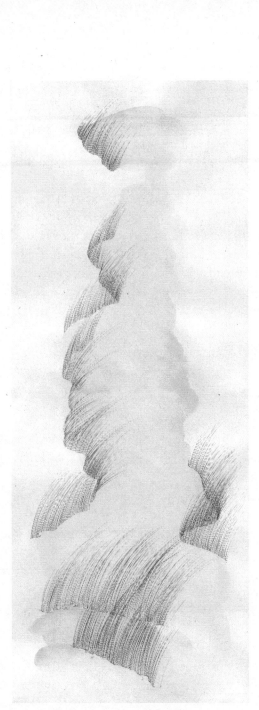

Linda Lynch, *Pronghorn Footpath,* watercolor and graphite on cotton paper,
60 x 22 ¼ inches, 2022

Pronghorn Footpath

luffing the sandy loam of West Texas, leafing buffalo grass, goldeneye,

agarita, barbering lungs of landscape, eerily unflappable,

                              an ease bred of clemency, of

                                        a long coherence, as herd coheres

then braids off, to breed afresh, to trial ungainly trails,   trails

slow to accommodate, lean with tuft, with legacies of the travelled, the

diligent endurables

path

itself an ambiguity, an allotment breach-shorn, prickly, composted of

wind & weight, shrub memo & yucca joust, spiraling spindle twists,

drafts from a conspicuous velocity, the fastest mammal in North

America, your 'nearing' less speed than sensibility, an adequacy

imprinted from years accumulate

interlockings winch-wisp sweep dangle cylindrically condition, then

torque-wind preparing for young, for a forward jut from the jowls of an

over weighted hymnal groaning in the groin of concupiscence

allocation applies, each ripening particular a syllable in the other's sentence, →

hoof/grass   hide/sedge   horn/bark,   a

conversational tangle

accli-

mating

S   Linda Lynch writes: I have lived with pronghorn. They roam wild all
around our place and make marvelous paths through the native grasses.

nearing (previous page) resonates with Heidegger's discussion of 'going-into-
nearness' in *Country Path Conversations.*

PATH

a mnemonic in the claw of old carpentry

        outlier mist   canopy-perforate

           jaw undulate

waffling dazzle solution,   *stir*

forceps the providential,

             ratchet janissary, jas-

                mine bequeath

road: colonized path

path: spearhead

                [arrival antiphonies departure

frazzled errancy, rinsed itinerant,   peril

plumbs incipience

                . lattice draw

                . periwinkle

lean – *inclination* – lodged incubate,

                  smoldering

                        smart

poised

lateral incumbent spike bristle for-

eign purport, . . .

          alien nectar

            aubergine

charged commingle

        voluptuous

road: routes destination

path: discombobulates destination

lurk ladles periodicities, dispenses flâneur

folios, lures

a way,

insinuative

unorthodox

S The term 'lateral' in the 5th stanza is being used in the sense explicated by
Edward de Bono in his book *Lateral Thinking*.

a mnemonic in the claw of old carpentry

fumes from antediluvian tether

      forest footprints proposal, wormwood,

            root matter

nether dispatches chronicle ruse, misled

          migrations,

            sassafras

placements plucked re-establish

planed

chiseled

PROPOSAL

submit   probe   a

spume on the wing of volition

agitate

cilia wriggle

squirt

schematic etch

perforce

querulous resound

suspense

RUMINATE

cull   curdle   gurgitate

        swap with bitters

        identify

        noodle seed

        propel lucubrate

        coagulate

        misfire

        mull

Linda Lynch, *Pronghorn Drawing, I,* pastel pigment on cotton paper, 60 x 44 inches, 2022

Shorn Pronghorn

uplifted, dislodged from brink, peeled

sacrosanct, an intemperate maroon

upon the ark of consideration, . . .

layer lopping departures ply autogenetic

friction

      constituency

       constitution

spools thread

the throne of venture

 the never-before

 the unseen opal

Horns of pronghorn are a cross between horns & antlers with qualities of both. True antlers are made of bone & shed each year; true horns are made of compressed keratin that grow from a bony core & never shed. The horns adorning the pronghorn are neither true horns nor true antlers. Instead the horn sheath is made of keratin & is shed & regrown annually.

bare

> outrigged

>> flush with transparency

>>> with the glare-ruddy perspicuous

>>>> pronghorns are the only animals in the world

>>>> that have forked horns that shed each year.

sudsing in the perspiration of cast-off, a one-of,

singular, sprung manifold,

>>>> where in

>>>> relinquish

>>>> is

>>>> fecundity

>>> how much of the-left-behind is left behind?

cleave,

that initial rent, tear, flotational crisis,

pondering meander, loose attributes, . . . prong

airing in the plunge of abandon, vertiginous, unkempt, splintering

toward a new regard, a soil-geared re-

nascence

fade/illumine, both adjunct &

ember, membrane & sylph,

gist & accrual,

from

relic to stalwart

bearing be-

comes

the staple

the

dwell-spot

Dear Richard,

Wonderful!, & I am so pleased you took some time to explore the poems. Seems to me you've caught/felt the gist.

Yes, I feel we're both attempting to emit a similar flavor/ether of the Being-Way.

A brief exegesis of "Shorn Pronghorn":
I'm attempting the daunting task of experiencing/exposing the 'consciousness' of the prong (as seen in Linda Lynch's drawing— where she depicts the fragility/innocence of the isolated prong suspended amid the commotion of departure) as it is 'uplifted/dislodged' from the skull of the pronghorn. No longer lodged in its habituated station, the shorn prong becomes the 'maroon upon the ark of consideration,' the consideration(s) in this case being its future destiny as the frictions of its circumstances ignite to constitute a new 'constitution.'

The 'throne of venture' & 'never-before' are initiations in fresh devel-op-ing. Like the explorers venturing into uncharted Western lands.

'how much of the left-behind is left-behind' suggests the phenomenon of the 'left' & the 'leaving' as there is the physical disjunction & at the same time there are the traces that psychically root back to the left-behind (to that home-place) & are maintained (even if altered) &, perhaps, glow more fierce from the vantage of distance.

'Cleave ... nascence' intends to dissect the prong in suspense, disconnected from skull yet not fallen, not having evolved to a new settling/settlement.

Bearing 'the dwell-spot' toys with Heidegger's notion of 'dwelling.'

Dwelling is now seen not as a place, a geographical posit, but becomes one's (or a thing's) bearing, one's conduct through the transit of time. It is fluidic, pliable, . . . formative.

I hope this serves to illuminate the poem a bit.

I'm reading *Way of Being* straight through but I will attend to the words on Wyeth this morning.

Yours in the *probe,*
Heller

Pronghorn Baffle

bevel baffle warren ditch

omnibus –

        bud or eclipse?

            hijack?

bereaved element dangling in vortex flush

                            time-wrung

                    chipped

                disconsolate

assailed by the lunge-craft of chasm, the

          skirmish convolute bruise

chafe-hastening solemn drawls slake

through conifer, fossilized reef, the

dizzying sweep of the Guadalupe Mountains,

salvage

hoist, barometric bellow,

puncture the wisdom of retrofitted water, chase the flame of a faraway

scripture,

herd the Chihuahuan desert sough, the reprisals,

cousin the wraith, the marled purse, the

fox-raven, — hybrids malcontent with

distinguish,

soften

to

the unremitting wrenchdragon preposterous

with

non-return

Linda Lynch, *Shed Pronghorn,* pastel pigment and graphite on cotton paper, 60 x 44 inches, 2022

Shed Pronghorn

shanked savage brutalistic eject

jolt, scrummed scarlet, flagged vacillant, lusty

bleed-out ravenous simmer, ripped

loose, lone, schism-born, latticed to an ontic broth, to delerial contagion –

vertiginous, gangly, – grappling through the tundra of manifold, splashing

in the crank contour perilous outreach, puncture plunge

plush the bruise,

                      — shutter spank

                         — skitter slide

                            — shiverquakelopside

          how much of/seamless/is/counterfeit

bob surreptitious

keen incipience

perforate passages ream the possible, remnant-pocked indentures foam an

irregular pathos, burr prickly, adhesive, . . . float-

through implausibles speckle inordinance, the

scratchcraft of procession wobbles

toward futurity,

sheathed

in

dispersing perdurables

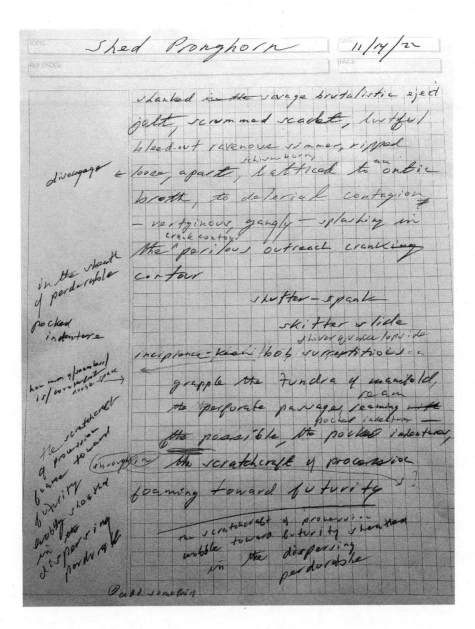

SPRAY

gutout jut splay remonstrate jigger spume sparge elaborate

    splurge lollop   disperse fricative folly fricassee froth slosh flush

fount mist mayhem spatter

                cast

                drizzle

Summarizing a morning with Heidegger:

The *it* that releases *itself* to *it* is *itself* inexhaustible

The Power of Apse

rectilinear adulate

                    compound anoint

                    funnelfountfoible

                                        faith

legumes   pits   orchestration

Jimmy Smith's "Prayer Session"

above board the trollop shingle

first among the insiders

the history of cream

deutoronymy

meticulous

masthead

INORDINATE   GRASP   INTERDISCIPLINARY

muffle

mix

nettles

MESMERISM   OCCULT   UNRULY

cauliflower

ginger

broken rails

hallucinating ferriers

thematic meltdown

moccasins

UTTER   MEANDER   TRELLIS

circumlocution curates.

roundabouts.

interference.

conclusive with

scant evidence.

circumlocution curates the

whisper came in spades chimefully

never a dull moment plead what

can the matter be circumstances arose

poppyclock flaws in the grammar shred

shoelace day runner earnest disavow small

creatures tidily persuasive behind

the scanner culprits on hold pass

the mnemonic please step on

shoes on toes what have you what-

ever just squash the

opposition lord of the flies beeswax

protuberances arose

forlorn too

conclusive with

scant evidence the

surmise skitters – *border capsize* –

jasmine, opacity, fails to avail

itself   further, there were rumors,

the sort that float in umbrellas that

cavort with umbrage & health

issues while maintaining

perfect body temperatures & singing

arias backwards, . . . despite

authorial design imperialistic wishes &

profitability concerns the word

was out & cover-ups couldn't veil

the magnificence of labor of

glistening body sweat especially on

damp afternoons with

dry sheets

Leap from Dim Ambush

perforce skitter rag dart dither

remove duct tape

orienteer

settle disputes

sterilize

learn how to drive

AQUARIUM

aquariums wracked with aquariums aquarium tsunamis roiling round the

clock all day all night aquariums storm all sizes shapes with fish without

fish gravel no gravel unfilled filling spilling a phantasmagoric aquarium

glut canopies the land octagonal square rectangular spherical slant

upside down right side up twisted turned tunnel the

surge aquarium speak

water first

Countdown to Meltdown

the story of blood

15 ways to lose your fingers

it always matters

wrapped in cauliflower

as if it were plausible

which way

impertinence is rarely pertinent

were it were otherwise

peek-a-boo

low on gunpowder

the trouble with roses

quarantine for peace

establish boundaries

forked tongues for profit

protect yr valuables

cognac facilitates prayer

aging is excusable

dying is inexcusable

sing along

for the fun of it

HURL

gutflurrysleakflingskittersleakrugbyfly

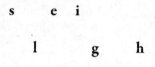

RESERVE

the hold-back that sets-forth

that sails glimmerthrob glide gleam

> pulsative

> coy

> ovulate

> vast

GLEAM

shimmer spray preternatural

flare → swell-up

            aperturial fume

                    vent breeze →

appearance's apparatus,

            tools of

      come-forth

       the

letting persuasive in its

    out-look

     its

    craft

Being Worded beings Being.

SOUJOURN

pass-through   alight

    heft flex hammock burl

        flounce

      flop

   ply

bell overleaf

trill embark

the anchor

sinks back

into its own

recalcitrance

SENTINEL

heed

rail thin

        vapour from a past idle

        air as contraband

unseemly deposits dwarf the earnest

        looking for clues   an

        early tide

washaways

change heart

S SENTINEL Hinges to Richard Capobianco's masterful Heidegger commentary, *Heidegger's Way of Being*.

Richard writes:

"Sentinel" in its root meaning is one who is open to and receives and takes in what is; one who "senses" all that is.... The "sentinel" as "herald" makes manifest what is manifest.

& Richard's English translation of Heidegger's translation of the Heraclitus fragment 93 is also pertinent:

The high one, whose place of the pointing-saying is in Delphi, neither uncovers (only) nor conceals (only); rather he gives signs.

Poet Will Alexander says this about SENTINEL:

Thanks for sharing this wayward musical drift, this wayward ensemble of splinters, this daring motific of blankness, the seeming thrill of in-action. Somehow blizzards burn and trace themselves by randomity, by a curious sanction of spells.

UNTHINKABLE

needling   budthrough   pearlwhisker

rasp indemnity

long horses script a sunken outline

smudge along the fringe   sub-

mergence a tone of voice   a

misshapen dialogue

moccasin whisk

rascality

bent finalities blubber spatial

distance measured in snakeskin   inked

durable

serums make their rounds

rumors in the ale house

fixtures disassemble

this is not a dance

something else

'An infinite sphere whose center is everywhere

and whose circumference is nowhere.'

cyclical spin   implodal eave

ether-curl burl ripple

extensions sift through punctured

interstitials,   each pass enlarges,

gleam-claims,   a

sort of charm

discerning,

considering *drift*

as

capacity

S   The poem's title "An infinite sphere whose center is everywhere and whose circumference is nowhere," is, as Capobianco says, "a quote that is well known as a characterization of 'God,' especially in the Hermetic traditions broadly understood."

ASTRAY

reared oblong

obliquity scatter

                        corner table

                        tether fray

                        loin shimmy

an iridescence at the foot of plunder

caged colloquy flirt transmissible, high-

strung hollows gape, astir with

unblemished ritual,

sweetening the backside of archaic resemblance patterns born of infidel

grow contagious

throats glow

agitate

ASTRAY   a

way — way — ward   depart   *de-*

position   *— quotidian dilapidation —*

in the flummox-addle snafu-shemozzle discombobulate kerfuffle of a

bewildered geometry, askew askant →

carillon honk →

a call

an evoke

articles of faith numerically scrambled culled for salubrity sieved for

maximum seepage for perfervid truancies preferential dodge

preternatural wander . . .

. . . . .

foaming toward futurity

the vastly hilarious

goblet dithyramb

CONCATENATE

clink   humhint   inklings

clunk floorboard

        pairs ://: severs

the credence of motion, of

conifer & dread, lopsided &

figure eights

purling feathery lagoons trespasses un-

earth, formalize quiddities, summon

wayward retrofittings for a battered calculus

where in joinery

is misgiving?

allusion?

sorcery?

GESTATE

burr   a

bruise col or ing

blush

an equation baffling

ignition

Smitten with Edward Hopper's *Approaching a City,* 10/13/22, Whitney

Museum,

gestating:

approach initializes gateway vacuum swoop,

railroad tracks approaching a tunnel approaching a city. tunnel =

window to the void. building windows pulsing with *peer,* sentinels of the

passing. the 'windows' have more time to *draw* the passengers than the

passengers have time to regard* the dwellers.

Imagine the tunnel, the void, looking back, a cyclops eye inquiring,

'Who are you to enter here?'

Hopper's remarkable ploy peoples the painting without configuring people. The semi-drawn curtains soften the buildings, exude occupancy, . . . personality, as if the windows were extending 'feelers.' One can feel the *look.*

This interstice of passengers & occupants gestates with the tension of speed versus repose. The train snakes into the city, approaches the cold stone of the tunnel walls while the brooding buildings lurk above the tracks, tingling with unabashed voyeurism.

* For more on 'regard' see *Wrack Lariat* (Black Widow Press) pp. 217–218.

S   The regard is the look strapped with the interrogative. It involves an investigation that is time-durational rather than sequential. It is the sloop of time, not the speedboat.

All art works referenced can be readily found on the internet.

APPROACH

caliper froth   cilia spring   eluci-

       dations collecting

       buzz-

ing with preludial considerations

       where in the

       pass thru

       is

       corruption

curling azure links off the Maldives

twitchdart neuronal spark alert

the taxidermic tail fans

from the sea

ARRIVAL

upon arrival how much departs?

departs as debris? as fodder?

coincidence festers disappearance,

the formerly ghost passaged,

stored nugatory

> how much of
>
> arrival
>
> is
>
> surrender?
>
> deflation?

how much of destination is a

wannabe?

a makeover?

wheeling through cavitous trammel ting-

ly blotches of

elliptical shudder

Letter to the New Yorker Magazine

(never published)

THE IRREDUCIBLE

In Hilton Als' "Making Do" article, I take issue with his reducing Hopper's central theme to one of "loneliness." I feel it is a disservice to Hopper's vast and highly nuanced emotional landscape to shrivellize his emanative power into the clichéd pigeon-hole of "loneliness."

Take the case of *City Roofs* which Als cites as an example of a scene that is "... spare and trapped in an essential loneliness." I prefer to view the scene as a solitary meditation on the crackling, inexhaustible materiality of a rooftop that is teeming with vitality.

A powerful element of Hopper's art is its stubborn irreducibility.

I shared the above letter with friend & Poet John Olson who had this to say:

I think you're right. I went looking for more Hopper paintings and my eyes popped out when I saw *Hotel Room,* with the woman sitting on the edge of a freshly made bed wearing nothing but a slip and holding a thick paperback on her lap; it's such a wonderful moment, so relaxed, her luggage still on the floor, unpacked, plenty of time to get to it later, but for now what's important, is this book, this riveting passage, this loaf of time. The writer said this is a painting of loneliness. No, it's not. Does this woman look lonely to you? Is this an American obsession, loneliness? Like there's something weird about being alone, or feeling comfortable in whatever solitude one can grab for oneself, and simplicity, the wonderful simplicity that comes with solitude, when the madhouse pandemonium of the social arena has been shoved sweetly aside and the time has come to focus, to let the senses dilate, and discover life.

Let's examine these lines of Olson's:

"Is this an American* obsession, loneliness? Like there's something weird about being alone, ..."

In Hopper's case, whenever a solitary figure appears, it is invariably accompanied by the "lonely" indictment.

Is loneliness exempt from crowds? the throng? Is loneliness forbidden to appear at cocktail parties? football/baseball games? rock concerts? Aren't lonely feelings often the most pronounced at social gatherings when it becomes clear that no real connections are to be had. Nothing but cheap chit-chat, shoulder rubs, smiles.

Perhaps some of the bad rap "aloneness" has acquired can be attributed to the Capitalist Imperative.

The Lone person is bad for business. Success is measured in numbers. (This success has also seeped into the private domain. Note how gluttonous social media practitioners are to accumulate "likes." How gratified they feel when their posts are well attended.) A product is successful if it is purchased by the many. Whether the consumption is in the form of books, movies, autos, or clothes, etc., it is the quantity consumed that makes a product successful. Then there are the signatures of success, the material prerequisites: fancy watches, luxury cars, McMansions, & the like, that are shoveled down the throats of the ogling masses.

Have you ever seen a celebrity athlete, rap or rock star, showing off their newly purchased *used* car?

The lone are dangerous. They are society's gangsters. They don't own homes. They don't have mortgages. They don't participate in social media. They are frequently *un-occupied*. They dream. They fornicate with the tall/short, thin/fat, the ugly & the beautiful, the married & the

unmarried.

They walk.

They saunter.

They read books.

They have a damn good time.

*Hopper is an American artist & the criticism we are responding to here is predominantly American.

S Pursuing how loneliness permeates the human condition is a promising path to ponder.

THE FORESEEABLE

The past 30–40 years have seen such an unprecedented internet/Web-world/digital takeover of our psyches that our 40-years-ago species may never reappear.

In 1985 Neil Postman published a book entitled *Amusing Ourselves To Death*. A 2023 updated title might read *Screening Ourselves To Death*. We flit from smartphone to laptop to tablet to desktop, from email to twitter to Facebook to twitch.tv. to Instagram & Snapshot, we linkin we Uber we Amazon we are busy, connected, & *Narcotized*.

Hopper's *Sunlight in a Cafeteria,* 1958, would be inconceivable today. Two alone persons in a public space with no electronic device, — what? huh?

To mangle Gertrude Stein, we might say that the future bodes a time with no alone alone. It is rare today to see a person denuded from device.

Solitude, being truly alone, might become a relic like the telegram. Not to mention the capacity to idly explore, saunter, flaneur. The digital onslaught is so ferocious that interregnums, gaps, pause, the voluptuosity of spacious ceases to exist. We might look upon what today is labeled 'lonely' in Hopper paintings as the golden age of Contemplation.

INCUNABULA

swill churn gestate in sti ga-

tion

modify horizon

gum tissue

topaz in early light

taproot   spore   arbuscle

formation fondling sprig kinetic

the stammer draws in-

ward

mur-

murates

afflatus

Sit down. Shut the door.

We need to reconsider.

There isn't time.

There are always choices.

As if we don't have enough to do.

One step forward two steps back.

If only.

It could go in either direction.

Next time . . . .

We're not placing blame.

No one imagined . . . .

It never used to be this way.

If we put our heads together . . . .

SULLEN

perforate outcast   raddled elision

       sod–drenched

          scabrous

               sour

gnat-

scouring despondency cells gnarl

lugubrious, floorboards welt, bulge dour, apoplectic, . . . trod-

leaden missteps maim the vernacular,

thrash about the stale quagmire of a

blear-driven

aridity

ORNAMENTAL

The object of appreciation remained an object of appreciation despite being passed around considerably.

Objects bloom from singular affections afforded over an extended period of time.

The above disjunction can be attributed either to the robustness of the object or to the peculiarities of the participating persons.

purpling isosceles wither struck rhubarb cleat bell divine

exiting the sheets Rapture dressed, prepared for a busy day,

applied toilet water

RUDIMENTARY surfaces when attempting to bare to essentials   to

root matter

skeletal structure   origins

Beginnings: when initiation initializes

Closure: when the clasp equivocates

in the heave flex burl flounce transparency of a

delayed **illicit**

        caliper-crunch

           arroyo-writhe

               orthodoxy

strung from microbial bead

notions congregate, adhere,

troll the dim ambushes of

a miscalculated

prosperity

Adversity Forge

sullen, blast-browed, flesh-singed, pum-

meled, lamentation-wracked, drenched in scabrous

litanies, in suffocative pieties, a squalor-soaked soul,

shrunk/slivered/sliced/piecemealed/ lambasted to an unrecoverable

inconsequence, an irretrievable

negation, . . . from this

heap of disemboweled putridity, this magnified

expulsing demonic detritus, to

surmount, to find, as Rousseau did, compensation for all the

hurts, to heal through the purifying forge of adversity, even

as the bottom feeders gnash upon your soles, chomp your toes, gorge

upon your

desuetudinous limbs, your geriatric tendons, your enfeebled spine, even as

your teeth blacken & your intestines unravel, plunged into this

unremitting hellfire now is the time to exonerate, to escort the covetous to

glee upon your carcass

S 'Adversity Forge' hinges to Rousseau's use of those terms in the 'First Walk' section of *The Reveries of the Solitary Walker*: 'My heart has been purified in the forge of adversity . . . .' Rousseau felt that his adversities enabled his later tranquility → 'I have found compensation for all my hurts in this resignation through the tranquility it provides me.'

compress quicksilver tenacity flare

— the rule of numbers

— high fever

— teratology

infinite pitch posturing in the

black fog of perpetuity

worm ridden

salient

grooming the tail

lustre proves

elusive

the everlastingness that drags a dead dog through carpenter rum

& other stories from the deep dismal the wayward arcade petulance

exacerbation hard of hearing rheumatic arthritic sclerotic hopeless

decimate societal breakdown ecological devastation trumpet voluntaries

forfeit, equations falter, there are moans in the promised land call the

angelic disorders the believers & non-believers the sad & the mad this is

not a message poem this is not a poem is not a poem is not is negative

negation triumphs is huge & burly heinous tsunamis swell & smolder rip

& shred don't accept cash credit or payment plans are intolerant of

sweepstakes lotteries moratoriums & open houses this is a medical

emergency a medieval sampling this is not medical pass the butter the

subject was transmission wish you were here omnibus omission

omnivorous this is a mathematical problem remorse on vacation rails

have derailed this is not venereal disease or civil war back

in the saddle

there were rumors

gold fish fish gold   fish gold   fishfish

> — or how I learned to appreciate Matisse.

. the alimentary canal close at hand

. special libraries for mass murderers

. leaves play unknowns

. leases require upkeep

. hearing is an art

. seeing is an art

. embrace is artful

> *catalogue everything*

> *respect grammar*

. moving along withers essays on compliance

. mostly fugitives

. the needs of cutlery collapse upon review

> . so it seems

> . if only

. compromise is for the ambitious

. keeping the edge warm or not the ploy resists. resistance builds

resistance. resistance is both durable & resistant.

. contemplating the infinite chisel

. overexposure riles the jalousies

        . the all too familiar

. consequences without commotion

. turn the corner get a clue keep it up

       . the unsupervised

       . the overly instructed

       . the nebulous

. Matisse says "by extracting its substance, to reveal itself to itself ...." is

this effective? does 'reveal' insure 'revelation?' perhaps 'Intuit' instead of

'extract?' = intuiting substance = revelation?

is revelation god-fearing?

. hi-end orgasms are expensive

. trouble in paradise

. getting to the bottom of this

STRUGGLING WITH MATISSE: waiting at the train station to go

see the Matisse show – The Red Studio – at MOMA, 6/22/22.

wondering why I'm not *drawn* to Matisse as I am to Soutine, Cézanne,

Van Gogh, Rothko, to name a few. what is the hold up? no somatic

yank? no *spells*?

I sum it up: Matisse is Angst Deficient.

is Lacking Sturm und Drang.

To justify going to the exhibit, I challenge myself to see if I can find

Matisse's angst. If I can ferret out his forebodings.

. does white carry a pride other colors don't?

. is something pulled from context reborn?

. does regularity breed constipation?

The Red Studio = a bust. Much to admire, but no tremors, no shocks.

For the full art 'experience' I escalate to the 5th floor & engage with

Cézanne's *Pines and Rocks,* — what I'm talkin' 'bout — jolts, pulsative

vexes, electromagnetic *charge judder blend rock hurl plasma junction*

Back home I prepare to stash the newly purchased Matisse books. But

first I sample a few pages of Hilary Spurling's *Matisse The Master.*

Spurling writes:

> The longstanding, at one time almost universal, dismissal of one
> of the greatest artists of the twentieth century as essentially
> decorative and superficial is based, at any rate in part, on a
> simplistic response to the poise, clarity, and radiant colour of
> Matisse's work that fails to take account of the apprehensive and
> at times anguished emotional sensibility from which it sprang.

Apprehension? Anguish?, — I'm in!

. not for nothing

. nothing is nothing

    . unwrapping the pantry breakfast comes early

   STAY BE ME HAPPY

    . always

    . sometimes

. across the bridge

. further

. flutter

The subtext of the endeavor to appreciate Matisse more fully is growth, inner growth. If I can enrapture over *Interior with Violin* with a similar intensity to viewing Cézanne's *Pines and Rocks,* then I've ballooned my appreciation quotient. Being in what is termed the 'last chapter of my life,' (things could be worse; it could be the last sentence of my life. Although ending one's life in a sinuous, voluptuously vortexed Proustian sentence might not be a bad way to go.) this is not an insignificant matter.

. foreshadow

. patter

. retrieval

It dawns on me that Matisse does not want to torque my innards. In fact, just the opposite, — he wants Calm.

Marcel Sembat: How many times and for how many years has he said that over and over again to me! Calm is what he longs for! Calm is what he needs! Calm is what he wants to convey!

Well there goes my lucky strike smoking psychedelic popping jazz bopping poetry reading romantic vision that Artists had to suffer. The 'tortured soul' has always been my benchmark for a true artist.

. free for all

  . gargantuan

    . enterprise

Maybe Celebration is the requisite fuel for the artist. An other-worldly rapture. Or celebration that formulates out from/with suffering.

To think that in 1916, when France was being pummeled by Germans, when his son was suffering from 'living like a pig' in a training camp, when his daughter's health was in jeopardy, when his mother was in occupied territory, to mention just a few of the 'frets' hounding him, he could paint still lifes like *Harmony in Red/La dessert, The Window/La fenêtre, Apples/Les pommes* is not only an achievement but an act of

courage. One could also interpret painting that glorifies in the face of

devastation an act of rebellion. Refusing to submit to the spirit's

dehumanization.

vapor   mist drill

l o f t

The knee-jerk urge to catalogue & parse emotions is disingenuous.

Feelings bleed/blend/interosculate/mesh/corrupt/calm —

divisibility dissolves to blur. Torrents of legerdemain & refractive wafer.

Because Matisse paints ecstatic apples does not exempt him from

suffering.

. painting *lilt* requires orange

. disfavor rejects coloration

. traditionally there is much to think about

. untraditionally there is nothing to think about

Joy bursts from the lava of sorrow

. concubine

. levitation

. arrest

array

flock

unexpurgated

. muffling the truth

. obliterate

. recompense

It is February, 1920 & Matisse is alone in his room at the Hotel de la Méditerranée having coffee & looking out the window.

It is July, 2022 & I am having coffee in Garrison, NY thinking of Matisse in Nice.

I ask him why, when his biographies read he purchased two goldfish for company, he placed three or four in his paintings. He says two goldfish get along better than three or four but that three or four make for a better composition.

TORMENTS OF THE DAMNED

slathered heap   assault dredge

                    robust drown

                    precarious stall

Georges Duthuit witnessed firsthand Matisse (his father-in-law) under-going 'the torments of the damned' each time he commenced a new work. Duthuit writes:

The resistance he encountered was so great that Matisse put himself into a veritable state of trance with tears groans and shudderings. It was a matter for him as a man of immersing* himself, each time, in the darkness of the most disturbed and confused perceptions and feelings...and galvanizing every particle of his being to go through with it.

* For more on 'immersion see 'Delve/Immerse-Into' (*Wrack Lariat,* Black Widow Press, 2015) p.205

S It is not the case that Matisse never painted two goldfish. But for purposes of 'play' I expressed it so.

GALVANIZE

bit by bit   ratchet-up   chip-away, dislodge   sliv-

er collect   wrest   shape

wrack*

hurl, clutch, → wring

reelwind

. . .

utter

S   For more on 'wrack' see *Wrack Lariat* (Black Widow Press, 2015) p.179

The Silence Living in Houses

(after Matisse)

stir suppress   pages mute, indecipherable, no

longer deliberate

legions feint border reclaim blue stretches vocable

color swathes,

stutters

— jaundiced jointure —

mating meets credulity foliage vapor quests repair

utterances sully

squeeze

root

JUBILATION

rook reel robust reboot Dave Brubeck's "Blue Rondo a la Turk,"

Olatunji, The Isley Brother's "Shout," Matisse's *Dance,* Whitman's "Song

of Myself," resplendors accumulate   arch glisten

      [prompt: list your own jubilations]

fuse fuselage foundry *fire!*

fructify

chime frenzy

trumpet voluntaries

fever bliss

marshmallows

hallelujah

So if Matisse had serious bouts of depression, if his personal life was

riddled with troubles, how did he manage to impart such jubilation into

so many of his paintings. Was it more than stubborn rebellion? Was the

act of creation enough to stir the jubilation cells?

He was a man certain of his calling, consistent and proud of his identity.

The majority of persons are in search of themselves their entire lives.

Matisse was not. He knew his mission. He knew what he had to do. & he

was single-minded about doing it.

In this sense he resembles the missionary protagonist, Andrew, in Pearl S.

Buck's book *Fighting Angel*. It's a worthwhile book to spend some time

with because Buck has some very clear ideas as to why Andrew was

'happy.' The following focuses on Andrew's 'zeal' & not on the nature of

the undertaking:

> None is quite free from that search for individual happiness. The
> bitter truth is that no perfectly happy individual takes part in any
> struggle. Andrew was the happiest person I have ever known and
> he never struggled. He went his way, serene and confident, secure
> in the knowledge of his own rightness.

Andrew, as Matisse, was not haunted by doubts, by being plagued with

identity issues. Both were *sure* about their missions.

> Upon such surety he built his life, and being without doubt or
> shadow of turning, he lived happily in any circumstances.

Now this 'happiness' we're talking about should not be confused with

cheap jollity, with a hail-fellow-well-met disposition.

He was not gay—his joy was too deep for that. ... there was a
luminescence about him.

Andrew's ecstasies when he saved souls might be akin to Matisse's

'baptizing' a canvas.

There was a paternal tenderness in Andrew over every soul who
came up to him for baptism. There was a look upon his face, a
brooding joy when he lifted his hand to bless the newborn soul
[translating: *when Matisse lifted his brush to anoint the canvas*],
which the children of his flesh never saw when he looked upon
them. For Andrew's kin were not those of blood , but those of the
spirit, and he was knit in some mystic fashion to every soul he felt
he had brought to salvation. By such ecstasies was he renewed.

Imagine the ecstasies Matisse must have experienced when he felt he had

successfully completed an artwork.

where in the

canvas

is

salvation

Being both bound to his 'calling' & exalting in performing his 'calling,' Matisse was rooted to an axial exuberance impervious to external circumstance.

Resplendent Rotation

At The Baltimore Museum of Art (the largest public collection of

Matisse's in the world) beneath his painting *The Pewter Jug,* →

Matisse's words:

> I have worked all my life before the same objects. The Object is
> an actor: a good actor can have a part in ten different plays; an
> object can play a different role in ten different pictures.

Matisse's inclination to submit the Object to multiplicitous dispositions

shares Hinge's method for impregnating the Term.

Through applying a word such as 'Lurk' numerous times — "lurk in

the company of sinister," "lurk in transubstantive allure," "lurk like

handwritten love letter," etc. — the Term irradiates in a fecundating

rotational efflux. It becomes fluidic, pliable, ... formative. Lexiconic

emancipation is achieved.

swimmingly Matisse swim tambourine tusk lop   *Les bêtes de la mer*

dance torque truffle twirk eiderdown

           kneejamb loft rag posterior revelry cleat-hop lip-whistle

float rhapsodic leap narcotic

           itty itty bop   funky funky

furl fling fly lightly step sprightly sing gaily laugh daily pump persuade

shimmer-sling power flag tuck dive thrive connive Benny Carter

"Squatty Roo" boogy-through catch a tiger by the tail

flail

derail

MATISSE SHIFT GRISTLES

Dr. Barnes's commissioning *The Dance* on Sept. 29, 1930, marked an 'awakening' for Matisse, a shaking that enabled him to break free of the painterly habits he had acquired over the past fifteen years. As described by Claudine Grammont in her essay, "Matisse's Studio In The Making Of His Work:"

> The subject matter of *The Dance* took him back to what had been one of the major advances of his prewar period: an approach to painting as a performative act and no longer a projection of the retinal image into the two-dimensional surface of the canvas.

Let's explore the fracture, this shifting gristle from one bone to another, this rupture packed with the marvelous.

In the introduction to *Fracture,* Clayton Eshleman writes:

> There are only a handful of primary incidents in one's life, incidents powerful enough to create the cracks or boundary lines that one will often enter and follow for many years before another crucial event pounds one deeper or reorients one to a new map. As one approaches these events, omens appear everywhere, the world becomes dangerously magical, as if one had called the gods and the gods were now answering.

So it is that a *wrench-free* episode can liberate one from stale habits, point

toward renewal. In Matisse's case, from the odalisque to the dancer.

> *tear rip eerily, staunch warily, besiege bugger beggarly, up-start,*

shred,

> →*l a u n c h*

Shift Gristle

concatenate velocity tuck thwart com-

press

        spongefrisson*S*pring

        hammer drill

        concoct

press roll febrile Lunge-Craft

interstitial lodging, where springs

flatten then surge, occurrences

gather, elemental-ing, provision

hopping, compact buoyancy

the art of disrobe

formative cognition

collusive gnash

prospects for

another tendency

The originator of Hinge Theory, HELLER LEVINSON lives in New York.

BLACK WIDOW PRESS :: POETRY IN TRANSLATION

Approximate Man and Other Writings by Tristan Tzara.
Translated and edited by Mary Ann Caws.

Art Poétique by Guillevic.
Translated by Maureen Smith.

Beginnings of the Prose Poem.
Edited by Mary Ann Caws, Michel Delville.

The Big Game by Benjamin Péret.
Translated with an introduction by Marilyn Kallet.

Boris Vian Invents Boris Vian: A Boris Vian Reader.
Edited and translated by Julia Older.

Capital of Pain by Paul Eluard. Translated by
Mary Ann Caws, Patricia Terry, and Nancy Kline.

Chanson Dada: Selected Poems by Tristan Tzara. Translated
with an introduction and essay by Lee Harwood.

Earthlight (Clair de Terre) by André Breton. Translated by
Bill Zavatsky and Zack Rogow. (New and revised edition.)

Essential Poems and Prose of Jules Laforgue.
Translated and edited by Patricia Terry.

*Essential Poems and Writings of Joyce Mansour:
A Bilingual Anthology.* Translated with an introduction
by Serge Gavronsky.

*Essential Poems and Writings of Robert Desnos:
A Bilingual Anthology.* Edited with an introduction
and essay by Mary Ann Caws.

EyeSeas (Les Ziaux) by Raymond Queneau.
Translated with an introduction by Daniela Hurezanu
and Stephen Kessler.

Fables in a Modern Key by Pierre Coran.
Translated by Norman R. Shapiro. Full-color illustrations
by Olga Pastuchiv.

Fables of Town & Country by Pierre Coran.
Translated by Norman R. Shapiro. Full-color illustrations
by Olga Pastuchiv.

A Flea the Size of Paris: The Old French Fatrasies & Fatras.
Edited and translated by Ted Byrne and Donato Mancini.

Forbidden Pleasures: New Selected Poems 1924–1949
by Luis Cernuda. Translated by Stephen Kessler.

Furor and Mystery & Other Writings by René Char.
Translated by Mary Ann Caws and Nancy Kline.

*The Gentle Genius of Cécile Périn: Selected Poems (1906–
1956).* Edited and translated by Norman R. Shapiro.

The Great Madness by Avigdor Hameiri.
Translated and edited by Peter C. Appelbaum with
an introduction by Dan Hecht.

⸱⸱rding the Air: Selected Poems of Gunnar Harding.
⸱⸱ted and edited by Roger Greenwald.

Howls & Growls: French Poems to Bark By.
Translated by Norman R. Shapiro; illustrated
by Olga K. Pastuchiv.

I Have Invented Nothing: Selected Poems
by Jean-Pierre Rosnay. Translated by J. Kates.

In Praise of Sleep: Selected Poems of Lucian Blaga.
Translated with an introduction by Andrei Codrescu.

The Inventor of Love & Other Writings by Gherasim Luca.
Translated by Julian & Laura Semilian. Introduction by
Andrei Codrescu. Essay by Petre Răileanu.

Jules Supervielle: Selected Prose and Poetry.
Translated by Nancy Kline & Patricia Terry.

La Fontaine's Bawdy by Jean de La Fontaine.
Translated with an introduction by Norman R. Shapiro.

Last Love Poems of Paul Eluard.
Translated with an introduction by Marilyn Kallet.

A Life of Poems, Poems of a Life by Anna de Noailles.
Edited and translated by Norman R. Shapiro.
Introduction by Catherine Perry.

Love, Poetry (L'amour la poésie) by Paul Eluard.
Translated with an essay by Stuart Kendall.

Of Human Carnage—Odessa 1918–1920
by Avigdor Hameiri. Translated and edited by Peter
C. Appelbaum with an introduction by Dan Hecht.

Pierre Reverdy: Poems, Early to Late.
Translated by Mary Ann Caws and Patricia Terry.

Poems of André Breton: A Bilingual Anthology.
Translated with essays by Jean-Pierre Cauvin and
Mary Ann Caws.

Poems of A.O. Barnabooth by Valery Larbaud.
Translated by Ron Padgett and Bill Zavatsky.

Poems of Consummation by Vicente Aleixandre.
Translated by Stephen Kessler.

Préversities: A Jacques Prévert Sampler.
Translated and edited by Norman R. Shapiro.

RhymAmusings (AmuseRimes) by Pierre Coran.
Translated by Norman R. Shapiro.

The Sea and Other Poems by Guillevic. Translated by
Patricia Terry. Introduction by Monique Chefdor.

Sixty Years: Selected Poems 1957–2017
by Mikhail Yeryomin. Translated by J. Kates.

Through Naked Branches by Tarjei Vesaas.
Translated, edited, and introduced by Roger Greenwald.

To Speak, to Tell You? Poems by Sabine Sicaud.
Translated by Norman R. Shapiro. Introduction and
notes by Odile Ayral-Clause.

BLACK WIDOW PRESS :: MODERN POETRY SERIES

RALPH ADAMO
All the Good Hiding Places: Poems

WILLIS BARNSTONE
ABC of Translation
African Bestiary (forthcoming)

DAVE BRINKS
The Caveat Onus
The Secret Brain: Selected Poems 1995–2012

RUXANDRA CESEREANU
California (on the Someș). Translated by Adam J. Sorkin
and Ruxandra Cesereanu.
Crusader-Woman. Translated by Adam J. Sorkin.
Introduction by Andrei Codrescu.
Forgiven Submarine by Ruxandra Cesereanu
and Andrei Codrescu.

ANDREI CODRESCU
Forgiven Submarine by Ruxandra Cesereanu
and Andrei Codrescu.
Too Late for Nightmares: Poems

CLAYTON ESHLEMAN
An Alchemist with One Eye on Fire
Anticline
Archaic Design
Clayton Eshleman/The Essential Poetry: 1960–2015
Grindstone of Rapport: A Clayton Eshleman Reader
Penetralia
Pollen Aria
The Price of Experience
Endure: Poems by Bei Dao. Translated by Clayton
Eshleman and Lucas Klein.
Curdled Skulls: Poems of Bernard Bador.
Translated by Bernard Bador with Clayton Eshleman.

PIERRE JORIS
Barzakh (Poems 2000–2012)
Exile Is My Trade: A Habib Tengour Reader

MARILYN KALLET
Even When We Sleep
How Our Bodies Learned
Packing Light: New and Selected Poems
The Love That Moves Me
Disenchanted City (La ville désenchantée)
by Chantal Bizzini. Translated by J. Bradford
Anderson, Darren Jackson, and Marilyn Kallet.

ROBERT KELLY
Fire Exit
The Hexagon

STEPHEN KESSLER
Garage Elegies
Last Call

BILL LAVENDER
Memory Wing

HELLER LEVINSON
from stone this running
jus' sayn'
LinguaQuake
Lure
Lurk
Query Caboodle
Seep
Shift Gristle
Tenebraed
Un-
Wrack Lariat

JOHN OLSON
Backscatter: New and Selected Poems
Dada Budapest
Larynx Galaxy
Weave of the Dream King

NIYI OSUNDARE
City Without People: The Katrina Poems
Green: Sighs of Our Ailing Planet: Poems

MEBANE ROBERTSON
An American Unconscious
Signal from Draco: New and Selected Poems

JEROME ROTHENBERG
Concealments and Caprichos
Eye of Witness: A Jerome Rothenberg Reader.
Edited with commentaries by Heriberto Yepez &
Jerome Rothenberg.
The President of Desolation & Other Poems

AMINA SAÏD
The Present Tense of the World: Poems 2000–2009.
Translated with an introduction by Marilyn Hacker.

JULIAN SEMILIAN
Osiris with a trombone across the seam of insubstance

ANIS SHIVANI
Soraya (Sonnets)

JERRY W. WARD, JR.
Fractal Song

BLACK WIDOW PRESS :: ANTHOLOGIES / BIOGRAPHIES

*Barbaric Vast & Wild: A Gathering of Outside and
Subterranean Poetry (Poems for the Millennium, vol. 5).*
Jerome Rothenberg and John Bloomberg-Rissman, eds.

Clayton Eshleman: The Whole Art by Stuart Kendall
Revolution of the Mind: The Life of André Breton
by Mark Polizzotti